Access
One step at a time

ALSO AVAILABLE

Access
One step at a time

by

N. Kantaris
and
P.R.M. Oliver

BERNARD BABANI (publishing) LTD.
THE GRAMPIANS
SHEPHERDS BUSH ROAD
LONDON W6 7NF
ENGLAND

PLEASE NOTE

© 1995 BERNARD BABANI (publishing) LTD

First Published - November 1995

British Library Cataloguing in Publication Data:

Kantaris Noel
Access - One step at a time
I. Title II. Oliver, Phil
005.7565

ISBN 0 85934 362 6

Printed and Bound in Great Britain by Cox & Wyman Ltd, Reading

ABOUT THIS BOOK

Access - One step at a time has been written to help users to store and retrieve information using this latest Windows database from Microsoft. No previous knowledge of database design is assumed.

The book does not describe how to install Microsoft Windows, or how to set up your computer's hardware, although some aspects of the Windows environment are described in Chapter 3. If you need to know more about these topics, then may we suggest that you select an appropriate level book for your needs from the 'Also Available' list - the books are graduated in complexity with the less demanding *One Step at a Time* series, followed by the *Concise Introduction* series, followed by the *Concise User's guide* series, to the more detailed *Explained* series. They are all published by BERNARD BABANI (publishing) Ltd.

The first chapter gives an overview of database systems and defines the elements that make up an Access relational database management system. The hardware and software requirements of your system are also discussed, so that you know in advance the minimum system configuration for the successful use of the package.

Below we list the major enhancements found in this latest version of Microsoft Access over the previous version. These are:

- The ability to display ToolTips to see button names.

- The ability to move and customise Toolbars.

- The ability to use shortcut menus with the use of the right mouse button.

- The use of Input Masks to facilitate data entry.

- The ability to use Best-fit Column Widths in a database table.

- The ability to print detailed information about the design of a database object.

- The ability to use the Table Wizards to choose from dozens of sample tables and hundreds of fields to help build your own tables.

- The ability to use the Query Wizards to create complex queries to help you to manage your data.

- The ability to define relationships between tables using the new Relationships window.

- The ability to create Forms and Reports in one keystroke.

- The use of an automatic Mail Merge facility with Word for Windows 6.

Most features of the package (old and new) will be discussed using simple examples that the user is encouraged to type in, save, and modify as more advanced features are introduced. This provides the new user with an example that aims to help with the learning of the most commonly used features of the package, and should help to provide the confidence needed to tackle some of the more advanced features later.

This book was written with the busy person in mind. It is not necessary to learn all there is to know about a subject, when reading a few selected pages can usually do the same thing quite adequately!

With the help of this book, it is hoped that you will be able to come to terms with Microsoft Access and get the most out of your computer in terms of efficiency, productivity and enjoyment, and that you will be able to do it in the shortest, most effective and informative way.

If you would like to purchase a Companion Disc for this or any of the listed books by the same author(s), containing the file/program listings which appear in them, then fill in the form at the back of the book and send it to P.R.M. Oliver at the stipulated address.

ABOUT THE AUTHORS

Noel Kantaris graduated in Electrical Engineering at Bristol University and after spending three years in the Electronics Industry in London, took up a Tutorship in Physics at the University of Queensland. Research interests in Ionospheric Physics, led to the degrees of M.E. in Electronics and Ph.D. in Physics. On return to the UK, he took up a Post-Doctoral Research Fellowship in Radio Physics at the University of Leicester, and then in 1973 a lecturing position in Engineering at the Camborne School of Mines, Cornwall, (part of Exeter University), where since 1978 he has also assumed the responsibility for the Computing Department.

Phil Oliver graduated in Mining Engineering at Camborne School of Mines in 1967 and since then has specialised in most aspects of surface mining technology, with a particular emphasis on computer related techniques. He has worked in Guyana, Canada, several Middle Eastern countries, South Africa and the United Kingdom, on such diverse projects as: the planning and management of bauxite, iron, gold and coal mines; rock excavation contracting in the UK; international mining equipment sales and international mine consulting for a major mining house in South Africa. In 1988 he took up a lecturing position at Camborne School of Mines (part of Exeter University) in Surface Mining and Management.

ACKNOWLEDGEMENTS

We would like to thank colleagues at the Camborne School of Mines for the helpful tips and suggestions which assisted us in the writing of this book.

TRADEMARKS

IBM and **PC-DOS** are registered trademarks of International Business Machines Corporation.

Intel is a registered trademark of Intel Corporation.

LaserJet is a registered trademark of Hewlett-Packard Company.

Microsoft, MS-DOS, and **Microsoft Windows** are registered trademarks of Microsoft Corporation.

PostScript is a registered trademark of Adobe Systems Incorporated.

Any other brand and product names are trademarks, or registered trademarks, of their respective companies.

CONTENTS

1. PACKAGE OVERVIEW

Microsoft Access is a database management system (DBMS) designed to allow users to store and retrieve information easily and quickly. A database is a collection of data that exists and is organised around a specific theme or requirement. It can be of the 'flat-file' type, or it can have relational capabilities, as in the case of Access, and is then known as a relational database management system (RDBMS).

The main difference between flat-file and relational database systems is that the latter can store and manipulate data in multiple 'tables', while the former systems can only manipulate a single table at any given time. To make accessing the data easier, each row (or **record**) of data within a database table is structured in the same fashion, i.e., each record will have the same number of columns (or **fields**).

We define a database and its various elements as follows:

Database	A collection of data organised for a specific theme in one or more tables.
Table	A two-dimensional structure in which data is stored, like in a spreadsheet
Record	A row of information in a table relating to a single entry and comprising one or more fields.
Field	A single column of information of the same type, such as people's names.

In Access the maximum number of tables in a database is limited to 128 and the maximum number of fields in a table to 256. However, the maximum number of records in a table is limited only by the capacity of your system.

A good example of a flat-file database is the invoicing details kept on clients by a company. These details could include name of client, description of work done, invoice number, and amount charged, as follows:

NAME	Consultancy	Invoice	Value
VORTEX Co. Ltd	Wind Tunnel Tests	9501	120.84
AVON Construction	Adhesive Tests	9502	103.52
BARROWS Associates	Tunnel Design Tests	9503	99.32
STONEAGE Ltd	Carbon Dating Tests	9504	55.98
PARKWAY Gravel	Material Size Tests	9505	180.22
WESTWOOD Ltd	Load Bearing Tests	9506	68.52

Such a flat-file DBMS is too limited for the type of information normally held by most companies. If the same client asks for work to be carried out regularly, then the details for that client (which could include address, telephone and fax numbers, contact name, date of invoice, etc., will have to be entered several times. This can lead to errors, but above all to redundant information being kept on a client - each entry will have to have the name of the client, their address, telephone and fax numbers.

The relational facilities offered by Access, overcome the problems of entry errors and duplication of information. The ability to handle multiple tables at any one time allows for the grouping of data into sensible subsets. For example, one table, called client, could hold the name of the client, their address, telephone and fax numbers, while another table, called invoice, could hold information on the work done, invoice number, date of issue, and amount charged. The two tables must have one unique common field, such as client reference number. The advantage is that details of each client are entered and stored only once, thus reducing the time and effort wasted on entering duplicate information, and also reducing the space required for data storage.

Hardware and Software Requirements

If Microsoft Access is already installed on your computer, you can safely skip the rest of this chapter.

To install and use Access, you need an IBM-compatible computer equipped with Intel's 80386sx (or higher) processor. The minimum recommended processor speed is 20 megahertz (MHz). In addition, you need a system with 6 megabytes (MB) of random-access memory (RAM), although 8MB are recommended, and a hard disc with 19MB of free space for a typical installation. You will also need the DOS operating system version 3.1 or later, and either the Windows 3.1, the Windows for Workgroups 3.11, the Windows 95, or the Windows NT environment.

Realistically, to run a reasonably sized Microsoft Access database with relational capabilities, you will need a 486 or a Pentium PC with preferably 8MB of RAM, with a VGA or higher display capability.

Although it is possible to operate Microsoft Access from the keyboard, the availability of a mouse is highly desirable. After all, pointing and clicking at an option on the screen to start an operation or command, is a lot easier than having to learn several different key combinations.

Installing Access

Installing Access on your computer's hard disc is made very easy with the use of the SETUP program, which even configures Access automatically to take advantage of the computer's hardware. You need to run the SETUP program because part of its job is to convert compressed Access files from the distribution discs prior to copying them onto your hard disc.

To install Access, start Windows, then use the Program Manager's **File, Run** command, as shown overleaf.

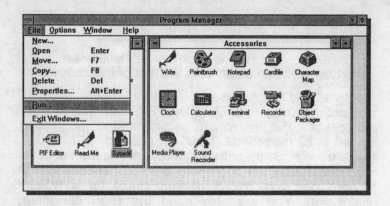

On selecting the command, the following dialogue box opens:

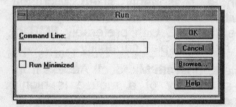

If the application was distributed on diskettes, insert disc #1 into the A: drive and type in the **Command Line** box

```
a:setup
```

Pressing the **OK** button, starts the installation of Microsoft Access. When a new disc is required, the installation program will inform you.

When all discs have been read, the SETUP program

will create and display a new group of icons, shown here, and will modify your system files automatically so that you can start Access easily. It even detects your computer's processor and display, and configures Access to run smoothly with your system.

2. STARTING ACCESS

To start Access you need to first start Windows. When the program is loaded, open the Windows Program Manager, and if you are using a mouse, point to the Access icon, shown here, and double-click the left mouse button.

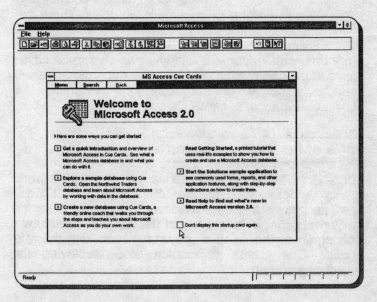

Microsoft Access

With the keyboard, after opening the Windows Program Manager, use the <Ctrl+Tab> key combination (while holding the <Ctrl> key down, press the <Tab> key), until the Microsoft Access Group is highlighted, then use the cursor keys to highlight the Access application icon, and press the <Enter> key.

The Welcome to Microsoft Access Screen

It is perhaps worth spending some time looking through the various parts of the MS Access Cue Cards that teach you about Microsoft Access.

For example, to **Get a quick introduction** point to the first 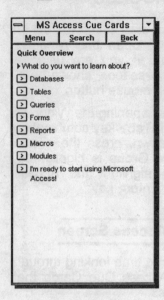 button and click the left mouse button. This opens up a new MS Access Cue Cards window with more options for you to choose from.

If you don't want the Cue Cards window to open next time you start Access, click at the small square at the bottom of the opening screen so that a large X appears in it.

If you are unfamiliar with the Windows environment, then read the rest of this chapter as well as the next one.

We use the word 'Windows' to refer to the whole Windows environment, while the word 'windows' refers to application (program) or document windows. There are two types of windows that can appear on your screen; the 'applications' windows which contain running programs, and 'document' windows which appear when applications can open more than one document (we will see an example of this shortly), but share the application window's menu.

Parts of the Access Screen

Some documents or applications you choose to work with in Access, such as the MS Access Cue Cards, open and use a separate window to display in. In order to illustrate the various parts of the Access screen, we look again at the Access opening screen with the MS Access Cue Cards application also displaying its welcoming screen.

6

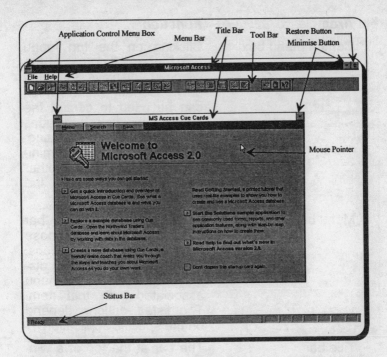

Application and document windows can have some common screen elements. However, not all windows use all of the available elements. For example, in the above two windows there are no scroll bars. These and other missing elements will be examined later.

Although more than one window can be displayed simultaneously, only one is the active window (which normally displays at the top of any other non-active windows, the exception being MS Access Cue Cards - to close it, press <Alt+F4>). Title bars of non-active windows appear a lighter shade than those of the active ones. In the above example, the Microsoft Access window is the active one. To activate the other window, click with the left mouse button anywhere within it.

The various screen areas have the following functions. These are described from the top of the screen, working from left to right.

Area	Function
Control menu box	Clicking on the top menu box (upper-left corner of the window), displays the pull-down Control menu which can be used to control the program window. It includes commands for re-sizing, moving, maximising, minimising, switching to another task, and closing the window.
Menu bar	The bar below the Title bar which allows you to choose from several menu options. Clicking on a menu item displays the pull-down menu associated with that item. The listed options depend on the specific application.
Title bar	The bar at the top of a window which displays the application name and the name of the current document.
Tool Bar	The bar below the Menu bar which contains buttons that give you mouse click access to the functions most often used in the program.
Restore button	Clicking on this button restores the active window to the position and size occupied before being maximised or minimised. The restore button is then replaced by a maximise button.

Minimise box	The button you point to and click to store an application as a small symbol at the bottom of the screen. Double clicking on such an icon will restore the screen.
Mouse pointer	The arrow which appears when the pointer is placed over menus, scrolling bars, buttons, and directory lists.
Status bar	The area at the lower-left corner of a window in which the current program status and present process is displayed.

Below we show additional screen elements not found in our previous screens:

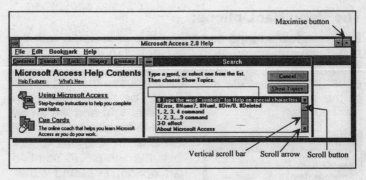

Maximise button	The button you point to and click to fill the screen with the active window. When that happens, the Maximise button changes to a Restore (vertical double-headed) arrow which can be used to restore the window to its former size.

9

Scroll bars	The bars on the extreme right and bottom of each window that contain a scroll box. Clicking on these bars allows you to see parts of a document that might not be visible in that size window.
Scroll arrows	The arrowheads at each end of each scroll bar at which you can click to scroll the screen up and down one line, or left and right one character, at a time.
Scroll boxes	The boxes on the Scroll bars that indicate the relative position of the visible part of the document with respect to the whole.

The Menu Bar Options:

Each window's menu bar option has associated with it a pull-down sub-menu, with the Control menu common to all applications. To activate the menu of a window, either press the <Alt> key, which causes the first option of the menu (in this case **File**) to be highlighted, then use the right and left arrow keys to highlight any of the options in the menu, or use the mouse to point to an option. Pressing either the <Enter> key, or the left mouse button, reveals the pull-down sub-menu of the highlighted menu option.

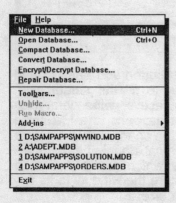

The sub-menu of the **File** option of the Microsoft Access window, is shown here.

Menu options can also be activated directly by pressing the <Alt> key followed by the underlined letter of the required option. Thus pressing <Alt+F>, causes the pull-down sub-menu of **F**ile to be displayed. You can use the up and down arrow keys to move the highlighted bar up and down a sub-menu, or the right and left arrow keys to move along the options in the menu bar. Pressing the <Enter> key selects the highlighted option or executes the highlighted command. Pressing the <Esc> key once, closes the pull-down sub-menu, while pressing the <Esc> key for a second time, closes the menu system.

Depending on what you are doing with Access, the items on the menu bar can be different from those of the opening screen. For example, when working with an existing database, or creating a new database, the menu options change to the ones shown below:

This is to be expected since available menu options reflect the type of work you are doing at the time. Similarly, the sub-menu under the **F**ile option of the above screen is different from the one of the Access opening screen. In general, menu options offer the following:

File   Produces a pull-down menu of mainly file related tasks, which allow you, amongst other things, to create a 'new' database, 'open' an existing database, 'rename' a database, 'print' a database, and 'exit' the program.

Edit   Produces a pull-down menu which allows you to 'undo' changes made, 'cut', 'copy' and 'paste' text.

11

Security	Allows you to specify the level of security required.
View	Allows you to view several database elements, such as 'tables', 'queries', 'forms', and 'reports'.
Window	Allows you to 'open' a new window, display multiple windows on your screen in 'cascade' or 'tile' form, or 'arrange icons' within an active window in a pre-determined spacing.
Help	Activates the help window and displays an 'index' of help or offers help on selected topics.

For a more detailed description of each sub-menu item, either highlight it and read the text on the status bar, or press **F1** to use the on-line **Help** system.

Dialogue Boxes

Three periods after a sub-menu option or command, means that a dialogue box will open when the option or command is selected. A dialogue box is used for the insertion of additional information, such as the name of a file.

To see a dialogue box, first point and click (once) on the Open Database icon, shown here. The Open Database dialogue box appears on the screen, as shown below:

When a dialogue box opens, the <Tab> key can be used to move the cursor from one field to another (<Shift+Tab> moves the cursor backwards), or alternatively you can move directly to a desired field by holding the <Alt> key down and pressing the underlined letter in the field name.

Within a group of options you can use the arrow keys to move from one option to another. Having selected an option or typed in information, you must press a command button, such as the **OK** or **Cancel** button, or choose from additional options. To select the **OK** button with the mouse, simply point and click, while with the keyboard, you must first press the <Tab> key until the dotted rectangle moves to the required button, and then press the <Enter> key.

The Open Database dialogue box, contains 'List' boxes which show a column of available choices, like the ones under **File Name** and **Directories**. If there are more choices than can be seen in the area provided for these lists, use the scroll bars to reveal them. To select a single item from a List box, either double-click the item, or use the arrow keys to highlight the item and press <Enter>.

Also note that this dialogue box contains List boxes that you need to open, such as the **List Files of Type** and **Drives**, by clicking at their respective down-arrow button. The same dialogue box contains 'Check' boxes which offer a list of options you can switch on or off. Selected options show a cross in the box against the option name, like the one against **Exclusive**.

Other dialogue boxes contain 'Option' buttons with a list of mutually exclusive items. The default choice is marked with a black dot against its name, while unavailable options are dimmed.

To cancel a dialogue box, either press the **Cancel** button, or the <Esc> key. Pressing the <Esc> key in succession, closes one dialogue box at a time, and eventually aborts the menu option.

Using Help in Access

The Access Help Program provides comprehensive on-line help. No matter what you are doing, pressing the F1 function key displays a help screen. For example, clicking the New Database icon to display the New Database dialogue box, then pressing the **F1** key, produces the right help window screen below. This window has been sized and moved from its original position, something you will learn to do in the next chapter.

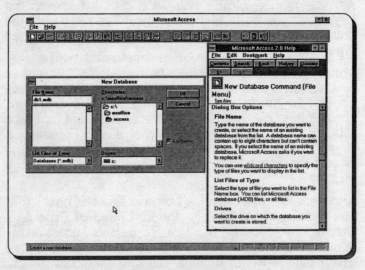

To close a Help window, or indeed any window, and return to your original screen, either double-click the window Control Menu Box (the large negative sign at the top left corner of the window), use <Alt+**F4**>, or use the **F**ile, E**x**it command from within that window.

Another way of getting context sensitive help is to double-click the Help button on the Tool bar, shown here, then move the modified mouse pointer to an Access menu option or to a given Tool bar button and click the left mouse button. This opens an appropriate help screen.

14

3. THE WINDOWS ENVIRONMENT

Microsoft Windows allows the display of multiple applications or multiple documents of a single application. Each of these Windows applications or documents, displays on the screen in its own window, which can be full screen size, part screen size, or reduced to an icon. Also, document windows of a single application can be tiled or cascaded on the screen for easy access.

The Mouse Pointers

In Access, as with all other graphical based programs, the use of a mouse makes many operations both easier and more fun to carry out.

Access makes use of the mouse pointers available in Windows, as illustrated below, which it uses for its various functions. When the program is initially started up the first you will see is the hourglass, which turns into an upward pointing hollow arrow once the Access screen appears on your display. Other shapes depend on the type of work you are doing at the time.

 The hourglass which displays when you are waiting while performing a function.

 The arrow which appears when the pointer is placed over menus, scrolling bars, and buttons.

I   The I-beam which appears in normal text areas of the screen.

 The large 4-headed arrow which appears after choosing the **Control, Move/Size** command(s) for moving or sizing windows.

The double arrows which appear when over the border of a window, used to drag the side and alter the size of the window.

The Help hand which appears in the help windows, and is used to access 'hypertext' type links.

Microsoft Access like other Windows applications, has additional mouse pointers which facilitate the execution of selected commands. These are:

The query pointer which appears on the screen after you click the Help button on the Tool bar. Pointing to a command name or an area on the screen and clicking, allows you to view a Help topic relating to the selected item.

The vertical pointer which appears when pointing over a column in a table and used to select the column.

The horizontal pointer which appears when pointing at a row in a table and used to select the row.

The slanted arrow which appears when the pointer is placed in the selection bar area of a table.

The vertical split arrow which appears when pointing over the area separating two columns and used to size a column.

The horizontal split arrow which appears when pointing over the area separating two rows and used to size a row.

Manipulating Windows

To use Access or any Windows program effectively, you will need to be able to manipulate a series of windows, to select which one is to be active, to move them, or change their size, so that you can see all the relevant parts of each one. What follows is a short discussion on how to manipulate windows.

To help with the illustration of the various points to be discussed shortly, we will create three windows in the 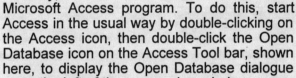 Microsoft Access program. To do this, start Access in the usual way by double-clicking on the Access icon, then double-click the Open Database icon on the Access Tool bar, shown here, to display the Open Database dialogue box, shown on the left of the screen dump below.

Microsoft distributes Access with an example database called **nwind.mdb** which is to be found in the **\sampapps** subdirectory. Selecting it and clicking the **OK** button displays the right window below.

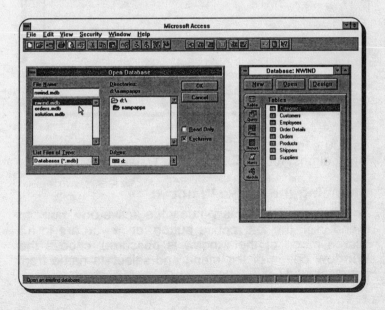

17

The screen dump of the previous page is a composite, showing both the Open Database dialogue box and the Database window which lists the tables that make up **nwind.mdb**. These two will not display simultaneously on your screen, as we have shown them in our screen dump, but we use this facility to avoid almost duplicate screen dumps, thus saving book space.

Next, double-click at the **Categories** table, which opens a Categories window, as follows:

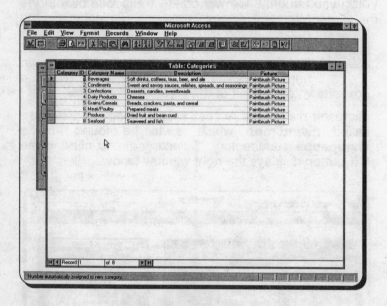

As you can see, the Categories window is such a size that it almost totally obscures the Database window.

Changing the Active Window:

To make the Database window the active one, point to it and click the left mouse button, or, if you are in full screen mode or the window is obscured, choose the **Window** option of the menu and select its name from the displayed list.

Next, having made the Database window the active one, double-click the **Customers** table to open a third window on your screen.

It is a good idea to practise what we are describing here by using the three newly created Access windows. Do not be afraid if you make mistakes - the more mistakes you make the more you will learn!

Moving Windows and Dialogue Boxes:

When you have multiple windows or dialogue boxes on the screen, you might want to move a particular one to a different part of the screen. This can be achieved with either the mouse or the keyboard, but not if the window occupies the full screen, for obvious reasons.

To move a window, or a dialogue box, with the mouse, point to the title bar and drag it (press the left button and keep it pressed while moving the mouse) until the shadow border is where you want it to be (as shown here), then release the mouse button.

To move a window with the keyboard, press <Alt+Spacebar> to reveal the Application Control menu, or <Alt+–> to reveal the Document Control menu. Then, press **M** to select **Move** which causes a four-headed arrow to appear in the title bar and use the arrow keys to move the shadow border of the window to the required place. Press <Enter> to fix the window in its new position or <Esc> to cancel the relocation.

Sizing a Window:

You can change the size of a window with either the mouse or the keyboard.

To size an active window with the mouse, move the window so that the side you want to change is visible, then move the mouse pointer to the edge of the window or corner so that it changes to a two-headed arrow, then drag the two-headed arrow in the direction you want that side or corner to move. Below we are moving the right side of the window towards the right, thus making the window larger. Continue dragging until the shadow border is the size you require, then release the mouse button.

To size a window with the keyboard, press <Alt+–> to reveal the Document Control menu, then press **S** to select **Size** which causes the four-headed arrow to appear, as shown here. Now press the arrow key that corresponds to the edge you want to move, or if a corner, press the two arrow keys (one after the other) corresponding to the particular corner, which causes the pointer to change to a two-headed arrow. Press an appropriate arrow key in the direction you want that side or corner to move and continue to do so until the shadow border is the size you require, then press <Enter> to fix the new window size.

An application window can only be sized if the application is not running in a maximised window. To size an application window, either use the mouse, or press <Alt+Spacebar> and continue as above.

Minimising and Maximising Windows:

A document window (or an application) can be

minimised into an icon at the bottom of the screen. This can be done either by using the mouse to click the 'Minimise' button (the downward arrow in the upper-right corner of the window), or by pressing <Alt+Spacebar> or <Alt+–> to reveal the Application Control menu or the Document Control menu, and

selecting **n** for **Mi_n_imise**.

In the above screen dump we show the Customers and Categories windows minimised at the bottom of the screen and the mouse pointer pointing at the minimise button of the Database window.

To maximise a window so that it fills the entire screen, either click on the 'maximise' button (the upward arrow in the upper-right corner of the window), or press <Alt+Spacebar> or <Alt+–> to display the Application Control menu or the Document Control menu, and select **x** for **Ma_x_imise**.

An application which has been minimised or maximised

can be returned to its original size and position on the screen by either double-clicking on its icon to expand it to a window, or clicking on the double-headed button in the upper-right corner of the maximised window, shown here, to reduce it to its former size.

With the keyboard, press <Alt+Spacebar> to display the Application Control menu, or <Alt+–> to display the Document Control menu, and select **R** for **_R_estore**.

Closing a Window:

A document window can be closed at any time to save screen space and memory. To do this, either double-click on the Control menu button (the large hyphen in the upper-left corner of the window, or press <Alt+-> and select **C** for **Close** from the Control menu.

If you try to close a window of an application document, such as that of the Categories table, in which you have made changes since the last time you saved it, you will get a warning in the form of a dialogue box asking confirmation prior to closing it. This safeguards against loss of information.

Windows Display Arrangement:

In Access, as with most other Windows application programs, you can display multiple windows in both tiled and cascaded (overlapping) forms - the choice being a matter of balance between personal preference and the type of work you are doing at the time.

On the next page we show the two forms of automatic display using the three windows we created earlier in Access. For the top screen dump, we used the **Window, Cascade** option, while for the bottom screen dump, we used the **Window, Tile** option.

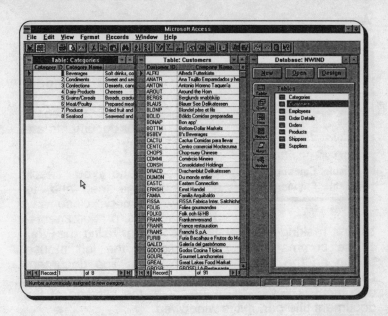

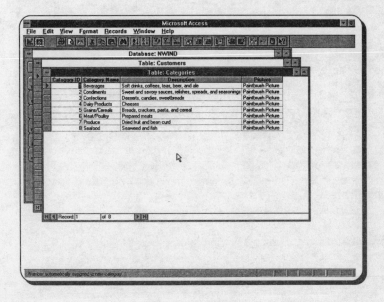

23

When you are using Access, or other Windows applications, it is very easy to open more files or documents than you need. Unless you check with the **Window** command, as shown here, you may not even know that some of these files or documents are open.

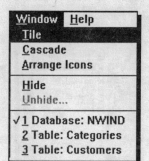

We recommend you check every now and then and, to conserve memory, close any unwanted files or documents, by first making them active, then either using the **File, Close** command, or double-clicking the left mouse button on the document control box. The document control box is at the left end of the menu bar, if the document is set to full page, or at the left end of the document title bar, if it is windowed.

4. DATABASE BASICS

To start designing a database using Microsoft Access, start Windows, then double-click at the Access icon, shown here. This opens the simple, two-menu option Access screen, with the **File** and **Help** options on the Menu bar. If the MS Access Cue Cards program loads, double-click the Application Control Menu Box, to close this application.

Next click the New Database icon, shown to the left, or use the **File, New Database** command, which causes the New Database dialogue box to be displayed, as follows:

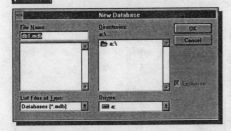

In the **File Name** box, type the database name, say Adept1, the program will insert automatically the **.mdb** extension. To avoid creating this database in the \ACCESS directory (the default directory chosen by Access), either select the \SAMAPPS subdirectory, or a working directory of your choice. We decided to save this example on a floppy disc, therefore we clicked the

down arrow against the **Drives** box, and selected the A: drive.

On pressing the **OK** button, the Database window, shown to the left, opens. It is from here that you can design the various elements that make up a database, such as Tables, Queries, Forms, and Reports.

Designing a Database Table

To design a database table, press the **New** button, which displays the New Table, shown below to the right of the Database window, with the two large buttons **Table Wizards** and **New Table**. The first allows you to automatically select from a list of pre-defined table applications, while the second allows you to start designing a table from scratch.

Clicking the **Table Wizards** button, opens the dialogue box shown at the lower right corner of the composite screen dump below.

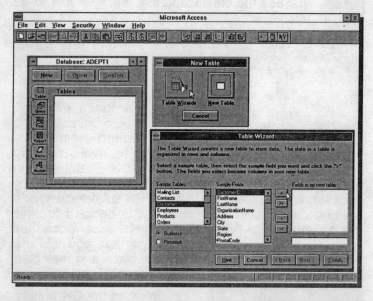

The database we are going to create holds the invoicing details which the firm Adept Consultants keep on their clients. One table will hold the details of the clients, while another will hold the actual invoice details, as described in Chapter 1. Therefore, we choose 'Customers' from the **Sample Tables** list of the Table Wizard dialogue box, which reveals a list of appropriate fields for that table.

26

You can either select all the fields or you can select a few. For our example, we selected the following fields: CustomerID, OrganizationName, Address, City, Region, PostalCode, ContactName, PhoneNumber and FaxNumber, by highlighting each in turn and pressing the 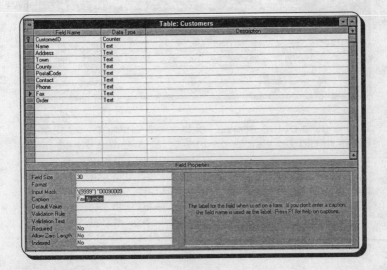 button.

Don't worry if these field names are not exactly what you want, as they can be changed easily. When you have selected all the required field names, press the **Finish** button, which displays the Customers Table ready for you to enter information.

Redesigning a Database Table:

To redesign the table, including changing its field names, click the Design View icon, or use the **View, Table Design** command, and edit the Field Name entries to those shown below. As each field name is highlighted, a Field Properties box appears at the bottom of the screen, in which you should also edit the name appearing against the Field Caption, or remove it altogether.

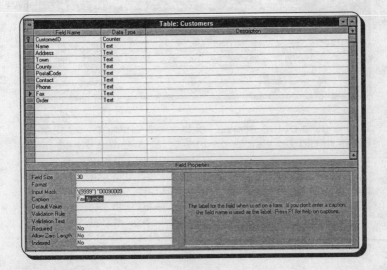

Next, place the cursor at the end of the Data Type descriptor of the CustomerID field which causes a down-arrow button to be displayed. Clicking this button, displays a drop-down list of data types, as shown here.

Field Name	Data Type
🔑 CustomerID	Counter
Name	Text
Address	Memo
Town	Number
County	Date/Time
PostalCode	Currency
Contact	Counter
Phone	Yes/No
Fax	OLE Object
Order	Text

As we intend to use the first four letters of a company's name as the CustomerID field, change the current data type from Counter to Text.

Finally, first click the Save icon (or use the **File, Save** command) to save your design changes, then click the Datasheet View icon (or use the **View, Datasheet** command) to revert to the Customers table so that you can start entering information, as shown below.

Customer ID	Name	Address	Town	County	Post Code	Contact
VORT	VORTEX Co. Ltd	Windy House	St. Austell	Cornwall	TR18 1FX	Brian Storm
AVON	AVON Construction	Riverside House	Stratford-on-Avon	Warwickshire	AV15 2QW	John Waters
BARR	BARROWS Associates	Barrows House	Bodmin	Cornwall	PL22 1XE	Mandy Brown
STON	STONEAGE Ltd	Data House	Salisbury	Wiltshire	SB44 1BN	Mike Irons
PARK	PARKWAY Gravel	Aggregate House	Bristol	Avon	BS55 2ZX	James Stone
WEST	WESTWOOD Ltd	Weight House	Plymouth	Devon	PL22 1AA	Mary Slim
GLOW	GLOWORM Ltd	Light House	Brighton	Sussex	BR87 4DD	Peter Summers
SILV	SILVERSMITH Co	Radiation House	Exeter	Devon	EX28 1PL	Adam Smith
WORM	WORMGLAZE Ltd	Glass House	Winchester	Hampshire	WN23 5TR	Richard Glazer
EALI	EALING Engines Design	Engine House	Taunton	Somerset	TN17 3RT	Trevor Miles
HIRE	HIRE Service Equipment	Network House	Bath	Avon	BA76 3WE	Nicole Webb
EURO	EUROBASE Co. Ltd	Control House	Penzance	Cornwall	TR15 8LK	Sarah Star

The widths of the above fields were changed so that all fields could be visible on the screen at the same time.

Customer ID	Name
▶ VORT	VORTEX Co. Ltd
AVON	AVON Construction
BARR	BARROWS Associates
STON	STONEAGE Ltd

To change the width of a field, place the cursor on the column separator until the cursor changes to the vertical split arrow, then drag the column separator to the right or left, to increase or decrease the width of the field.

Sorting a Database Table

As you enter information into a database table, you might elect to change the field headings by clicking the Design Table icon and editing the Field Name entries. If you do this, on return to the Customers table you will find that the records have sorted automatically in ascending order of the entries of the field in which you left the cursor while in the Design Table.

Contact	Phone	Fax	Order
Brian Storm	01776-223344	01776-224466	1
John Waters	01657-113355	01657-221133	2
Mandy Brown	01554-664422	01554-663311	3
Mike Irons	01765-234567	01765-232332	4
James Stone	01534-987654	01534-984567	5
Mary Slim	01234-667755	01234-669988	6
Peter Summers	01432-746523	01432-742266	7
Adam Smith	01336-997755	01336-996644	8
Richard Glazer	01123-654321	01123-651234	9
Trevor Miles	01336-010107	01336-010109	10
Nicole Webb	01875-558822	01875-552288	11
Sarah Star	01736-098765	01736-098567	12
			(Counter)

If you want to preserve the order in which you entered your data, then add an Order field as the last field of your database table, and select its data type as Counter. This can be done at any time, even after you finished entering all other information in your table.

Sorting a database table in ascending order of a Counter type field, results in the database table displaying in the order in which the data was originally entered in that table. Above, we show the Contact field, so that you can cross-check the original order of your Customer table, as well as the rest of the information in that table not shown in the screen dump of the previous page.

To sort a database table in ascending or descending  order of the entries of any field, place the cursor in the required field and click the Ascending or Descending icon, shown here.

With the keyboard, select the **Records, Quick Sort** command, then choose either the **Ascending** or the **Descending** option.

29

Applying a Filter to a Sort:

If you would like to sort and display only records that fit selected criteria, then click the Edit Filter/Sort icon, shown here, or use the **Records, Edit Filter/Sort** command, which opens the Filter dialogue box, shown below.

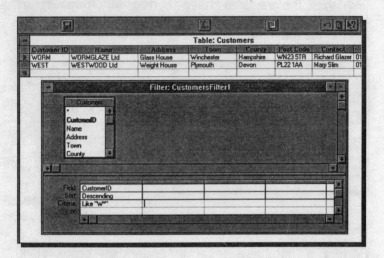

The upper portion of the dialogue box displays all the fields in the Customers table, while the lower portion is where you enter your filter restrictions. In the above example, we chose to view, in ascending order, the records within the CustomersID field that start with W - we typed W* and Access displayed *Like "W*"*.

On pressing the Filter Sort icon (shown here top left), the Customers table displays with only two entries, as seen in the above composite screen dump. To revert to the display of all the records, press the Show All Records icon (shown here bottom left).

To obtain extensive help on the subject, including an Examples screen, use the Query Pointer on the Filter dialogue box, then select Sorting and Filtering Records, followed by Entering Criteria in a Query or Criteria.

Using a Database Form

Once a table has been selected from the Database window, clicking the AutoForm icon, shown here, or using the **View Form** command, automatically displays each record of that table in form view. The created form. for the Customers table is shown below.

A form can be used to enter, change or view data. They are mainly used to improve the way in which data is displayed on the screen.

Forms can also be used to sort records in a database table in ascending or descending order of a selected field.

When you attempt to close a Form window, you will be asked whether you would like to save it. An Access database can have lots of different forms, each designed with a different purpose in mind. Saved forms are displayed in the Database window when you press the Form button, as shown here.

In a later chapter we will discuss Form design in some detail, including their use for adding and retrieving data.

Working with Data

Adding Records in a Table:

Whether you are in Table view or Form view, to add a record, click the New icon, shown here.

When in Table view, the cursor jumps to the first empty record in the table (the one with the asterisk in the box to the left of the first field). When in Form view, Access displays an empty form which can be used to add a new record.

Finding Records in a Table:

Whether you are in Table or Form view, to find a record click the Find icon, or use **Edit, Find**. This opens the following dialogue box:

Note the field name on the Title bar, which is CustomerID, indicating that the cursor was on the CustomerID field before we clicked the Find icon or selected the **Find** command.

To find all the records starting with **w**, we type **w*** in the **Find What** box of the dialogue box and we search the **Current Field**. The **Current Field** option can be changed to **All Fields**, if you so wish. However, leaving it as it is and pressing the **Find First** button, highlights the first record with the CustomerID "WEST", as you can see from the composite screen dump above. Pressing the **Find Next** button, highlights the next record that matches our selected criteria.

Deleting Records from a Table:

To delete a record when in Table view, point to the box to the left of the record to highlight the entire record, as shown below, then press the <Del> key.

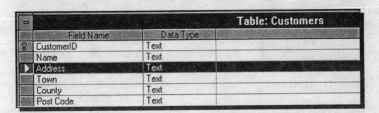

	WEST	WESTWOOD Ltd	Weight House	Plymouth	Devon	PL22 1AA
	WORM	WORMGLAZE Ltd	Glass House	Winchester	Hampshire	WN23 5TR
*						

To delete a record when in Form view, first display the record you want to delete, then use the **Edit, Select Record** command to select the whole record, and press the <Del> key.

In both cases you will be given a warning and you will be asked to confirm your decision.

Delete, Insert, and Move Fields in a Table:

To delete a field from a table, close any forms that might be open, then load the table from the Database window, then press the Design View icon, click the row selector to highlight the field you want to remove, as shown below,

	Field Name	Data Type	
🔑	CustomerID	Text	
	Name	Text	
▶	Address	Text	
	Town	Text	
	County	Text	
	Post Code	Text	

Table: Customers

and press the Delete Row icon, shown here, or use the **Edit, Delete Row** command.

To insert a field in a table, display the table in Design View, and highlight the field above which you want to insert the new field, and press the Insert Row icon, shown here, or use the **Edit, Insert Row** command.

To move a field from its current to a new position in a table, select the field you want to move, then point to the row selector so that the mouse pointer is inclined as shown below, and drag the row to its new position.

	Field Name	Data Type	
🔑	CustomerID	Text	
	Name	Text	
	Address	Text	
	Town	Text	
	County	Text	
	Post Code	Text	
►	Contact	Text	
	Phone	Text	
	Fax	Text	

Note that while you are dragging the field, the mouse pointer changes to the one pointing at the Name field in the above composite. Releasing the mouse button, moves the Contact field to where the Name field is now and pushes all other fields one row down.

Printing a Table View:

You can print a database table by clicking the Print

icon, or you can preview it on screen by clicking the Preview icon.

However, printing directly from here, produces a pre-defined print-out, the format of which you cannot control effectively. For example, the selected range in the Print dialogue box, must be contiguous. Also, even though you can choose to print in portrait or landscape form by pressing the **Setup** button, you cannot control the printed font size.

For a better method of producing a printed output, see the Report Design section.

5. RELATIONAL DATABASE DESIGN

In order to be able to discuss relational databases, we will add to the current database an Orders table.

Open the Adept1 database and use the **New** button on the Database window to add an Orders table to it. Use the **Table Wizards** and select Orders from the displayed **Sample Tables** list. Next, select the five fields displayed below under **Fields in my new table** from the **Sample Fields** list, and press the **Next** button.

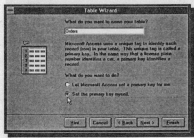

This displays the dialogue box shown here, in which you can, if you want to, change the name of the table.

Click the 'Set the primary key myself' option and press the **Next** button to select OrderID as the key field.

The key field must be unique in a table, and the OrderID field satisfies this requirement. This field is used by Access for fast searches.

Now press the **Next** button and click the **Numbers and/or letters I enter when I add new records** option shown on the adjacent dialogue box. Finally, press the **Finish** button.

Next, use the Design Table facility, as discussed in the previous chapter, to change the Data Types of the selected Field Names to those displayed below.

	Field Name	Data Type	Table: Orders
🔑	OrderID	Text	
	CustomerID	Text	
▶	EmployeeID	Text	
	OrderDate	Date/Time	
	ShipDate	Date/Time	

The information you need to enter in the Orders table is shown below.

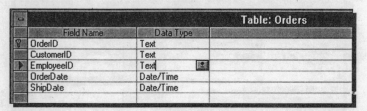

	Order ID	Customer ID	Employee ID	Order Date	Ship Date
▶	94085VOR	VORT	A.D. Smith	20/03/95	10/04/95
	94097AVO	AVON	W.A. Brown	25/03/95	14/04/95
	94099BAR	BARR	S.F. Adams	01/04/95	02/05/95
	95002STO	STON	C.H. Wills	20/04/95	25/05/95
	95006PAR	PARK	A.D. Smith	13/05/95	16/06/95
	95010WES	WEST	W.A. Brown	15/05/95	26/06/95
	95018GLO	GLOW	L.S. Stevens	25/06/95	19/07/95
	95025SIL	SILV	S.F. Adams	28/06/95	22/07/95
	95029WOR	WORM	C.H. Wills	20/07/95	13/08/95
	95039EAL	EALI	A.D. Smith	30/07/95	25/08/95
	95045HIR	HIRE	W.A. Brown	18/08/95	08/09/95
	95051EUR	EURO	L.S. Stevens	25/08/95	19/09/95
	95064AVO	AVON	S.F. Adams	20/09/95	15/10/95
*					

Record: 1   of 13

Relationships

Information held in two or more tables of a database is normally related in some way. In our case, the two tables, Customers and Orders, are related by the CustomerID field.

 To build up relationships between tables, return to the Database window and press the Relationships icon on the Tool bar, shown here. This opens the following window in which the index field in each table is emboldened.

You can build relationships between tables by dragging

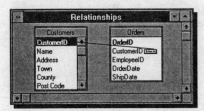

a field name from one table into another. In our example, we have dragged CustomerID from the Customers table (by pointing to it, pressing the left mouse button, and while keeping the mouse button pressed, dragging the pointer) to the required field in the other table, in this case CustomerID in the Orders table. Releasing the mouse button opens the following dialogue boxes (the second one by pressing the **Join Type** button on the first one).

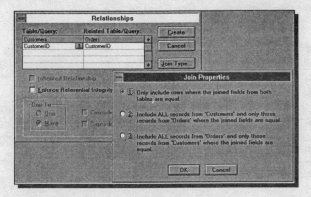

On the Join Properties dialogue box you can specify the type of join Access should create in new queries - more about this later. For the present, press the **OK** button on the Join Properties dialogue box, to close it, then check the **Enforce Referential Integrity** box in the Relationships dialogue box, and press the **Create** button. Access creates and displays graphically the chosen type of relationship in the Relationships window shown here.

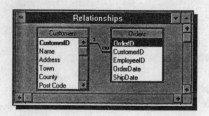

Note the relationship "1 customer to many (∞) orders" symbolism in the Relationships window.

Type of Relationships:

Because Access is a relational database, data can be used in queries from more than one table at a time. As we have seen, if the database contains tables with related data, the relationships can be defined easily. Usually, the matching fields have the same name, as in our example of Customers and Orders tables. In the Customers table, the CustomersID field is the primary field and relates to the CustomersID field in the Orders table - there can be several orders in the Orders table from one customer in the Customers table.

Inherited Relationships
If you attach tables from another Access database and select the **Inherited Relationship** option in the Relationships dialogue box, the original relationships of the attached database are displayed for you to use in your current database. If you clear relationships in your current database, this does not affect the original relationships in the attached database.

Referential Integrity

Selecting the **Enforce Referential Integrity** option in the Relationships dialogue box, helps to ensure that relationships between records are enforced according to certain rules, when you add or delete records in related tables. The related tables must belong to the same database.

The rules, when referential integrity is enforced, are:

- You can only add records to a related table, if a matching record already exists in the primary table. For example, you cannot add records in the Orders table of our example, unless the related customer exists in the Customers table.

- You cannot delete a record from the primary table if matching records exist in a related table. For example, you cannot delete a customer from the Customers table, if related orders exist in the Orders table.

The last restriction can be overcome by setting the Cascade Delete/Update options in the Relationships dialogue box. The effect is as follows:

If the **Cascade Delete Related Records** option is set, deleting a record from the primary table, automatically deletes related records in the attached table(s). For example, deleting a customer from the Customers table, automatically deletes all orders relating to this customer from the Orders table - a useful but dangerous option!

If the **Cascade Update Related Fields** option is set, any changes you make to the primary key values causes Access to automatically make necessary changes to the related fields in the attached table(s). For example, if you change the CustomerID in the Customers table, the change is automatically reflected in all records in the Orders table - a very useful option.

Viewing and Editing Relationships

To view the current relationships between tables in a database, activate the Database window and press the Relationships icon. This displays the now familiar Relationships window.

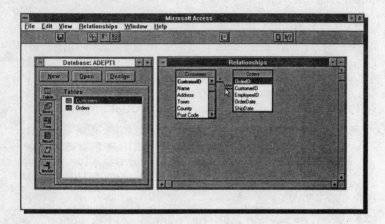

To edit a relationship, double-click the left mouse button at the position shown on the above screen dump. The tip of the mouse pointer must be on the inclined line joining the two tables in the Relationships window, as shown, before Access will respond. If you have difficulty with this action, first point to the relationship line and click once to embolden it, then use the **Relationships, Edit Relationship** command. Either of these two actions will open the Relationships dialogue box in which you can change the various options already discussed.

A given relationship can easily be removed altogether, by first activating it (pointing and clicking to embolden it), then pressing the <Del> key. A confirmation dialogue box will be displayed. To delete a table, you must first detach it from other tables, then select it in the Database Window and press the <Del> key. Think before you do this!

Creating an Additional Table

As an exercise, create a third table using the **Table Wizards** and select Invoices from the displayed **Sample Tables** list. Next, select the five fields displayed below - the names and their data types have been changed using the Design Table facility.

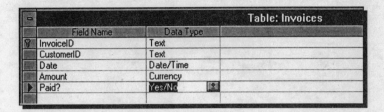

	Table: Invoices	
Field Name	Data Type	
InvoiceID	Text	
CustomerID	Text	
Date	Date/Time	
Amount	Currency	
Paid?	Yes/No	

Next, enter the data given below and build up appropriate relationships between the Invoices table, the Customers table and the Orders table, as shown overleaf.

Invoice No	Customer ID	Date	Amount	Paid?
AD9501	VORT	10/04/95	£120.84	No
AD9502	AVON	14/04/95	£103.52	Yes
AD9503	BARR	02/05/95	£99.32	No
AD9504	STON	25/05/95	£55.98	No
AD9505	PARK	16/06/95	£180.22	No
AD9506	WEST	26/06/95	£68.52	No
AD9507	GLOW	19/07/95	£111.56	No
AD9508	SILV	22/07/95	£123.45	Yes
AD9509	WORM	13/08/95	£35.87	No
AD9510	EALI	25/08/95	£58.95	No
AD9511	HIRE	08/09/95	£290.00	No
AD9512	EURO	19/09/95	£150.00	No
AD9513	AVON	15/10/95	£135.00	No

The relationships between the three tables should be arranged as follows:

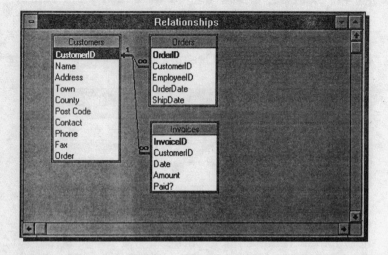

It is important that you should complete the above exercise, as it consolidates what we have done so far and, in any case, we will be using all three tables in what comes next.

6. CREATING A QUERY

You create a query so that you can ask questions about the data in your database tables. For example, you could find out whether you have more than one order from the same customer in our Adept database.

Before carrying on, use Windows' File Manager to copy **adept1.mdb** to **adept2.mdb**. We suggest you do this fairly frequently to make a backup of your database, in case a file gets corrupted. Next, start Access, load Adept1, and in the Database window click the **Query** button, followed by the **New** button which displays the New Query dialogue box.

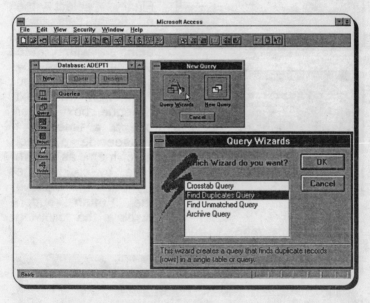

Next, click the **Query Wizards** button which opens the Query Wizards dialogue box, shown in the composite screen dump above, and select the **Find Duplicates Query** option. On clicking **OK**, the Find Duplicates Query Wizards dialogue box is displayed, as shown on the next page.

From the displayed database tables in this dialogue box, select the Orders table and press the **Next** button.

On the following dialogue box select **CustomerID** as the field you want to check for duplicate values, then press the [>] button, followed by the **Next** button.

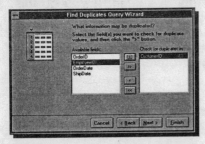

Finally, select the additional fields you would like to see along with the duplicate values, by selecting those you want from the next dialogue box, either one at a time or, if you decide to select all of them, as shown here, by clicking the [>>] button. Clicking the **Finish** button displays the following

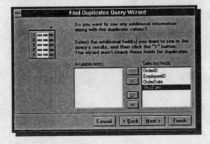

Select Query screen.

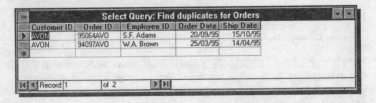

Customer ID	Order ID	Employee ID	Order Date	Ship Date
AVON	95064AVO	S.F. Adams	20/09/95	15/10/95
AVON	94097AVO	W.A. Brown	25/03/95	14/04/95

Record: 1   of 2

If you examine the original Orders table, you will indeed find that it contains two orders from AVON.

Types of Queries

The query we have created so far, is known as the *Select Query*, which is the most common type of query. However, with Access you can also create and use other types of queries, as follows:

- **Crosstab query** - used to present data with row and column headings, just like a spreadsheet. It can be used to summarise large amounts of data in a more readable form.

- **Action query** - used to make changes to many records in one operation. For example, you might like to remove from a given table all records that meet certain criteria, make a new table, or append records to a table. Obviously, this type of query has to be treated with care!

- **Union query** - used to match fields from two or more tables.

- **Pass-through query** - used to pass commands to an SQL (see below) database.

- **Data-definition query** - used to create, change, or delete tables in an Access database using SQL statements.

SQL stands for Structured Query Language, often used to query, update, and manage relational databases. Each query created by Access has an associated SQL statement that defines the action of that query. Thus, if you are familiar with SQL, you can use such statements to view and modify queries, or set form and report properties. However, these actions can be done more easily with the QBE (query-by-example) grid, to be discussed next. If you design union queries, pass-through queries, or data-definition queries, then you must use SQL statements, as these type of queries can not be designed with the QBE grid. Finally, to create a subquery, you use the QBE grid, but you enter an SQL SELECT statement for criteria, as we shall see in the next QBE grid example.

The Query Window

The Query window is a graphical query-by-example (QBE) tool. Because of Access' graphical features, you can use the mouse to select, drag, and manipulate objects in the query window to define how you would like to see your data.

An example of a ready made Query window can be seen by selecting the Find duplicates for Orders query and clicking the **Design** button on the Database window. This action opens the Select Query dialogue box shown below.

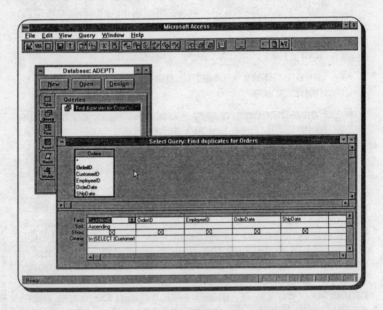

You can add a table to the top half of the Query window by simply dragging the table from the Database window. Similarly, you can add fields to the bottom half of the Query window (the QBE grid) by dragging fields from the tables on the top half of the Query window. In addition, the QBE grid is used to select the sort order of the data, or insert criteria, such as SQL statements.

46

To see the full SQL SELECT statement written by Access as the criteria selection when we first defined the query, widen the width of the first field, as follows:

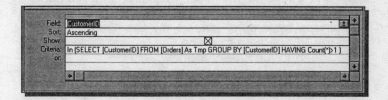

Note the part of the statement which states 'As Tmp GROUP'. Access collects the data you want as a temporary group, called a *dynaset*. This special set of data behaves like a table, but it is not a table; it is a dynamic view of the data from one or more tables, selected and sorted by the particular query.

Creating a New Query:

Below, we show a composite screen created by clicking the **New** button on the Database window, then clicking the **New Query** button on the New Query dialogue box. This opens both the Select Query and the Add Table dialogue boxes. The Invoices and Customers tables were then added to the Select Query window.

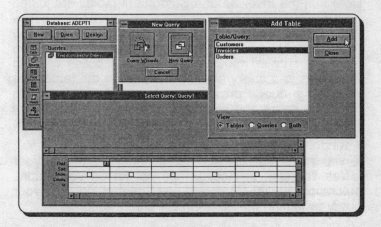

47

Adding Fields to a Query Window:

Below we show a screen in which the Paid? and InvoiceID fields have been dragged from the Invoices table and added to the Query window. In addition, the Name and Contact fields have been dragged from the Customers table and placed on the Query window, while the Phone field from the Customers table is about to be added to the Query window.

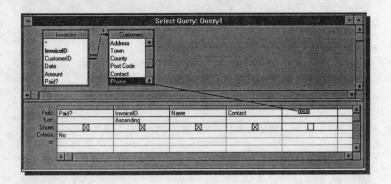

Having dragged all five fields from the two tables onto the QBE grid, we have added the word No as the criteria on the Paid? field and selected Ascending as the Sort for the InvoiceID field.

Note that the Invoices and Customers tables are joined by a line that connects the two CustomerID fields. The join line was created when we designed the tables and their relationships in the previous chapter. Even if you have not created these relationships, Access will join the tables in a query automatically when the tables are added to a query, provided each table has a field with the same name and a compatible data type and one of those fields is a primary key. A primary field is displayed in bold in the Query window.

If you have not created relationships between your tables yourself, or Access has not joined your tables automatically, you can still use related data in your query by joining the tables in the Query window.

Pressing the Run icon on the Tool bar, shown here, instantly displays all the unpaid invoices with the details you have asked for, as follows:

	Paid?	Invoice No	Name	Contact	Phone
▶		AD9501	VORTEX Co. Ltd	Brian Storm	01776-223344
	No	AD9503	BARROWS Associates	Mandy Brown	01554-664422
	No	AD9504	STONEAGE Ltd	Mike Irons	01765-234567
	No	AD9505	PARKWAY Gravel	James Stone	01534-987654
	No	AD9506	WESTWOOD Ltd	Mary Slim	01234-667755
	No	AD9507	GLOWORM Ltd	Peter Summers	01432-746523
	No	AD9509	WORMGLAZE Ltd	Richard Glazer	01123-654321
	No	AD9510	EALING Engines Design	Trevor Miles	01336-010107
	No	AD9511	HIRE Service Equipment	Nicole Webb	01875-558822
	No	AD9512	EUROBASE Co. Ltd	Sarah Star	01736-098765
	No	AD9513	AVON Construction	John Waters	01657-113355
*					

Select Query: Unpaid Invoices

Record: 1   of 11

To save your newly created query, use the **File, Save Query As** command, and give it a name such as 'Unpaid Invoices'.

Types of Criteria:

Access accepts the following expressions as criteria:

Arithmetic Operators		Comparison Operators		Logical Operators	
*	Multiply	<	Less than	And	And
/	Divide	<=	Less than or equal	Or	Inclusive or
+	Add	>	Greater than	Xor	Exclusive or
-	Subtract	>=	Greater than or equal	Not	Not equivalent
		=	Equal	Eqv	Equivalent
		<>	Not equal	Imp	Implication

Other operators		
Between	Between 50 And 150	All values between 50 and 150
In	In("Bath","Bristol")	All records with Bath and Bristol
Is	Is Null	All records with no value in that field
Like	Like "Brian *"	All records with Brian something in field
&	[Name]&" "&[Surname]	Concatenates strings

Combining Criteria

By specifying additional criteria in a Query window you can create powerful queries for viewing your data. In the examples below we have added the field Amount to our Unpaid Invoices query.

The AND Criteria with Different Fields:

When you insert criteria in several fields, but in the same row, Access assumes that you are searching for records that meet all of the criteria. For example, the criteria below list the following records:

Field:	Paid?	Amount	InvoiceID	Name	Contact	
Sort:			Ascending			
Show:	☒	☒	☒	☒	☒	
Criteria:	No	Between 50 And 150			Like "M*"	
or:						

Select Query: Unpaid Invoices

Paid?	Amount	Invoice No	Name	Contact	Phone
No	£99.32	AD9503	BARROWS Associates	Mandy Brown	01554-664422
No	£55.98	AD9504	STONEAGE Ltd	Mike Irons	01765-234567
No	£68.52	AD9506	WESTWOOD Ltd	Mary Slim	01234-667755

The OR Criteria with the Same Field:

If you include multiple criteria in one field only, then Access assumes that you are searching for records that meet any one of the specified criteria. For example, the criteria <50 or >100 in the field Amount, shown below, list the required records, only if the No in the Paid? field is inserted in both rows.

Field:	Paid?	Amount	InvoiceID	Name	Contact	
Sort:			Ascending			
Show:	☒	☒	☒	☒	☒	
Criteria:	No	<50				
or:	No	>100				

50

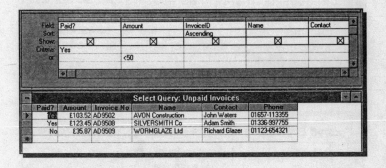

Paid?	Amount	Invoice No	Name	Contact	Phone
►	£120.84	AD9501	VORTEX Co. Ltd	Brian Storm	01776-223344
No	£180.22	AD9505	PARKWAY Gravel	James Stone	01534-987654
No	£111.56	AD9507	GLOWORM Ltd	Peter Summers	01432-746523
No	£35.87	AD9509	WORMGLAZE Ltd	Richard Glazer	01123-654321
No	£290.00	AD9511	HIRE Service Equipment	Nicole Webb	01875-558822
No	£150.00	AD9512	EUROBASE Co. Ltd	Sarah Star	01736-098765
No	£135.00	AD9513	AVON Construction	John Waters	01657-113355

The OR Criteria with Different Fields:

If you include multiple criteria in different fields, but in different rows, then Access assumes that you are searching for records that meet either one or the other of the specified criteria. For example, the criteria Yes in the Paid? field and the criteria <50 in the Amount field, but in different rows, list the following records.

Field:	Paid?	Amount	InvoiceID	Name	Contact
Sort:			Ascending		
Show:	☒	☒	☒	☒	☒
Criteria:	Yes				
or:		<50			

Paid?	Amount	Invoice No	Name	Contact	Phone
►	£103.52	AD9502	AVON Construction	John Waters	01657-113355
Yes	£123.45	AD9508	SILVERSMITH Co	Adam Smith	01336-997755
No	£35.87	AD9509	WORMGLAZE Ltd	Richard Glazer	01123-654321

The AND and OR Criteria Together:

The following choice of criteria will cause Access to retrieve either records that have Yes in the Paid? field and the company's name starts with the letter A, or records that the invoice amount is less than £50.

Field:	Paid?	Amount	InvoiceID	Name	Contact
Sort:			Ascending		
Show:	☒	☒	☒	☒	☒
Criteria:	Yes			Like "A*"	
or:		<50			

51

The retrieved records from such a query are shown below.

Paid?	Amount	Invoice No	Name	Contact	Phone
Yes	£103.52	AD 9502	AVON Construction	John Waters	01657-113355
No	£35.87	AD 9509	WORMGLAZE Ltd	Richard Glazer	01123-654321

Using Wildcard Characters in Criteria:

In the previous example we used the criteria A* to mean any company whose name starts with the letter A. The asterisk in this criteria is known as a wildcard character.

To search for a pattern, you can use the asterisk (*) and the question mark (?) as wildcard characters when specifying criteria in expressions. An asterisk stands for any number of characters, while a question mark stands for any single character in the same position as the question mark.

The following examples show the use of wildcard characters in various types of expressions:

Entered Expression	Meaning	Examples
a?	Any two-letter word beginning with A	am, an, as, at
???d	Any four-letter word ending with d	find, hand, land yard
Sm?th	Any five-letter word beginning with Sm and ending with th	Smith Smyth
fie*	Any word starting with the letters fie	field, fiend, fierce, fiery
*ght	Any word ending with ght	alight, eight, fight, light, might, sight
*/5/95	All dates in May '95	1/5/95

Creating Calculated Fields

Let us assume that we would like to increase the amounts payable on all invoices overdue by more than 30 days from today by 0.5%, as a penalty for not settling an account on time. We can achieve this by creating a calculated field in our database.

To create a calculated field, open Adept1, click the Query button on the Database window, double-click the Unpaid Invoices query, and click the Design View button on the Tool bar. Next, insert a field after the Amount field using the **Edit, Insert Column** command, and type in the Field row of the newly inserted empty column, the following information:

```
New Amount:[Amount]*1.005
```

where *New Amount:* is our chosen name for the calculated field - the colon is essential. If you do not supply a name for the calculated field, Access uses the default name *Expr1:*, which you can rename later. The square brackets enclosing the word Amount in the above expression indicate a field name.

 Next, click the Properties button, shown here, or use the **View, Properties** command, to set the Format property to Currency.

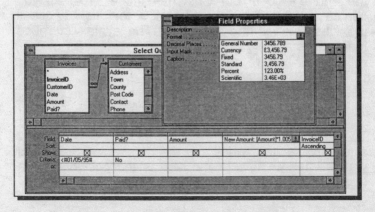

53

Finally, add the Date field from the Invoices table to our query and type the expression <#01/05/95# in its Criteria field - the hash marks and leading zeros are supplied by Access if you do not type them yourself.

Clicking the Datasheet View button on the Tool bar, displays the following screen:

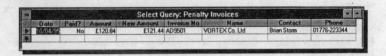

We suggest you save this query under the name Penalty Invoices.

Using Functions in Criteria

There are several functions that you can use in a calculated field of an Access query which can either be applied to extract information from a text field or date fields, or be used to calculate totals of entries.

Finding Part of a Text Field:

Let us assume that you want to find information that is part of a text field, like the area code (first 5 numbers) in the Phone field of our Customers table. To help you search a table for only part of a text field, Access provides three string functions. The syntax of these functions is as follows:

```
Left(stringexpr,n)
Right(stringexpr,n)
Mid(stringexpr,start,n)
```

The *stringexpr* argument can be either a field name or a text expression, while *n* is the number of characters you are searching for, and *start* is the position of the first character you want to start from.

Thus, to extract the area code of the text field Phone in our Customers table, we would type in the Field row of an empty field, either

```
Area Codes:Left([Phone],5)
```
or
```
Area Codes:Mid([Phone],1,5)
```

Note that to distinguish between the name of a field and a text expression, the name of the field is enclosed in square brackets.

The result of such a query is displayed below:

Paid?	Amount	Invoice No	Name	Contact	Phone	Area Codes
No	£120.84	AD9501	VORTEX Co. Ltd	Brian Storm	01776-223344	01776
No	£99.32	AD9503	BARROWS Associates	Mandy Brown	01554-654422	01554
No	£55.98	AD9504	STONEAGE Ltd	Mike Irons	01765-234567	01765
No	£180.22	AD9505	PARKWAY Gravel	James Stone	01534-987654	01534
No	£68.52	AD9506	WESTWOOD Ltd	Mary Slim	01234-667755	01234
No	£111.56	AD9507	GLOWORM Ltd	Peter Summers	01432-746523	01432
No	£35.87	AD9509	WORMGLAZE Ltd	Richard Glazer	01123-654321	01123
No	£58.95	AD9510	EALING Engines Design	Trevor Miles	01336-010107	01336
No	£290.00	AD9511	HIRE Service Equipment	Nicole Webb	01875-558822	01875
No	£150.00	AD9512	EUROBASE Co. Ltd	Sarah Star	01736-098765	01736
No	£135.00	AD9513	AVON Construction	John Waters	01657-113355	01657

Finding Part of a Date Field:

To extract part of a date field, such as the month in which unpaid invoices were issued, type

```
Month:DatePart("m",[Date])
```

in the Field row of an empty field.

To extract the year in which unpaid invoices were issued, type

```
Year:DatePart("yyyy",[Date])
```

in the Field row of an empty field. This function returns the year in four digits, such as 1995.

Calculating Totals in Queries:

It is possible that you might want to know the total value of outstanding invoices grouped by month. Access allows you to perform calculations on groups of records using *totals* queries, also known as *aggregate* queries.

The table below lists the functions that can be used in

queries to display totals. These functions are entered in the Totals row of a query which can be displayed by clicking the Totals button, shown here, while in Design View.

Function	Used to Find
Avg	The average of values in a field
Count	The number of values in a field
First	The field value from the first record in a table or query
Last	The field value from the last record in a table or query
Max	The highest value in a field
Min	The lowest value in a field
StDev	The standard deviation of values in a field
Sum	The total of values in a field
Var	The variance of values in a field

Below we show the one-table query to find the total of values of unpaid invoices grouped by month.

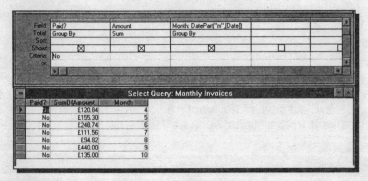

56

7. ADVANCED QUERIES

We have seen in the last chapter how to create a query with fields taken from two tables. The query in question was the Unpaid Invoices, shown below in Design View.

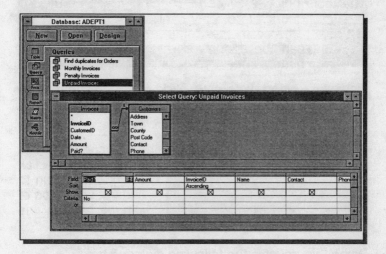

In order to make it easy for us to know which field in the

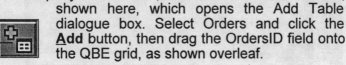

above query comes from which table, we clicked the Table Names button on the tool bar, shown here. This adds the Table row in the QBE grid.

Now, suppose we would like to add the Orders table so that we can see the OrdersID field in extracted records of our query. To do this, click the Add Table button, shown here, which opens the Add Table dialogue box. Select Orders and click the **Add** button, then drag the OrdersID field onto the QBE grid, as shown overleaf.

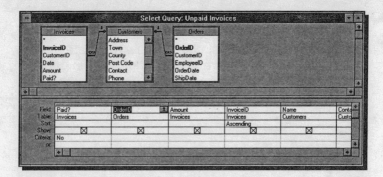

However, when you now click the Datasheet View button on the Tool bar to see the extracted records, Access displays the following message:

To correct this error, double-click the offending join to find out what type of join we have in this case.

Doing this, reveals the following dialogue box:

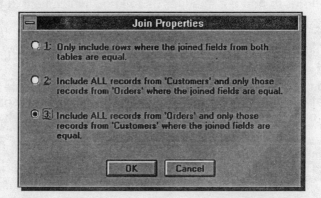

Obviously, option 3 is the wrong join. What we really need, is option 2. Select it to extract the correct records.

58

Types of Joins

Microsoft Access supports the following types of joins:

Types of joins	Effect
Equi-joins or Inner joins	A join in which records from two tables are combined and added to a dynaset only when there are equal values in the joined fields. For example, you can find records that show orders placed by each customer, with the dynaset containing only records for customers who have placed orders.
Outer joins	A join in which all the records from one table are added to the dynaset, and only those records from the other table for which values in the joined fields are equal. For example, you can find records that show all customers together with any orders they have placed.
Self-joins	A join in which records from one table are combined with other records from the same table when there are matching values in the joined fields. A self-join can be an equi-join or an outer join.

For an inner join, select option 1 from the Join Properties dialogue box. For an outer join, select option 2 or 3, depending on which records you want to include.

For example, choosing option 2 (also called a *left outer join*), in the case of our previous example, displays all the required records from the Customers table and only those records from Orders where the joined fields are equal. Option 3 (also called a *right outer join*), on the other hand, attempts to display all records in Orders and only those records from Customers where the joined fields are equal, resulting in some confusion in our particular example.

Creating a Parameter Query

A *Parameter Query* is a variation of the *Select Query* - the type we have been using so far. A Parameter Query is used when you frequently run the same query, but change the criteria each time you run it. Instead of having to make changes to the QBE grid, the design of a Parameter Query causes Access to prompt you for criteria. This type of query is particularly useful when used as a filter with forms.

To design a Parameter Query, design a **New** query in the normal way (do not use the Query Wizards), or change an existing Select Query. We have chosen the latter route and selected to change the Penalty Invoices query. In Design View, this now looks as follows:

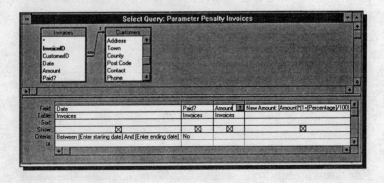

Note the two changes made to the above query. In the Date field we have entered two prompts (in square brackets) in the Criteria row, namely

```
[Enter starting date]
[Enter ending date]
```

and in the calculated field we have replaced the *1.005 by

```
*(1+[Percentage]/100)
```

60

Running this query, causes Access to ask for input values on three successive Enter Parameter Value boxes, as shown in the composite screen dump below:

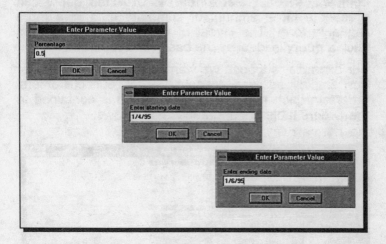

Providing the appropriate input information, displays the result of the search, as follows:

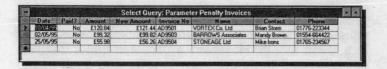

We have saved this query under the name Parameter Penalty Invoices.

Creating a Crosstab Query

You create a *Crosstab Query* to display totals in a compact, spreadsheet format. A Crosstab query can present a large amount of summary data in a more readable form. The layout of the extracted data from such a query is ideal as the basis for a report.

For example, suppose we wanted to examine which of our employees was responsible for our customers' orders in each month. The information is contained in the Orders table of our database as follows:

From the way this information is presented it is very difficult to work out who was responsible for which order in a given month. However, a Crosstab query that lists the names of the employees in rows and each month as a column heading, would be an ideal way to present this type of information.

To create a Crosstab query, open the Adept1 database and click first the Queries button, then the **New** button on the Database window. Next, click the **Query Wizards** button on the New Query dialogue box and choose **Crosstab Query** from the list of Wizards in the Query Wizards dialogue box, as shown on the composite screen dump on the next page.

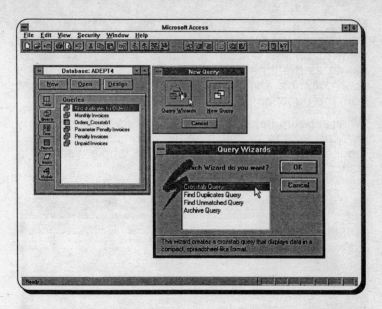

Pressing the **OK** button, causes the Crosstab Query Wizard dialogue box to appear on the screen. Select Orders from the displayed list of tables and press the **Next** button.

From the next dialogue box, select a maximum of three

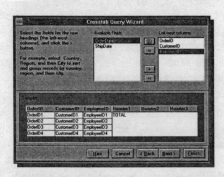

fields from the displayed list, which will become the row headings of the crosstab form. Choose OrderID, CustomerID, and EmployeeID, in that order, as shown here. The order you select these fields is important as Access will list the results of the query in alphabetical order of the first selected field.

63

Having selected the three fields, click the **Next** button, and choose the OrderDate as the field whose value you want to be the column headings. Press **Next**, select Month as the time interval by which you want to group your columns and press **Next**. Finally, choose Count from the Function list and press **Finish**.

What appears below is the result of this Crosstab query with the widths of the monthly columns appropriately reduced so that you can see the whole year at a glance.

Order ID	**Customer ID**	**Employee ID**	**Row Summary**	**Jan**	**Feb**	**Mar**	**Apr**	**May**	**Jun**	**Jul**	**Aug**	**Sep**	**Oct**	**Nov**	**Dec**
94085VOR	VORT	A.D. Smith	1	1											
94097AVO	AVON	W.A. Brown	1	1											
94099BAR	BARR	S.F. Adams	1			1									
95002STO	STON	C.H. Wills	1			1									
95006PAR	PARK	A.D. Smith	1					1							
95010WES	WEST	W.A. Brown	1					1							
95018GLO	GLOW	L.S. Stevens	1						1						
95025SIL	SILV	S.F. Adams	1						1						
95029WOR	WORM	C.H. Wills	1							1					
95039EAL	EALI	A.D. Smith	1							1					
95045HIR	HIRE	W.A. Brown	1									1			
95051EUR	EURO	L.S. Stevens	1									1			
95064AVO	AVON	S.F. Adams	1											1	

Record: 1 of 13

As you can see from the above screen dump, the required information is tabulated and extremely easy to read. However, the displayed recordset is not updatable.

To see the underlying structure of the query, click the Design View button to display the QBE grid, as follows:

Field:	OrderID	CustomerID	EmployeeID	Expr1: Format([OrderDate],"mmm")	The Value: OrderDate	Row Summary: OrderDat
Table:	Orders	Orders	Orders		Orders	Orders
Total:	Group By	Group By	Group By	Group By	Count	Count
Crosstab:	Row Heading	Row Heading	Row Heading	Column Heading	Value	Row Heading
Sort:					Row Heading	
Criteria:					Column Heading	
or:					Value	
					[not shown]	

If you want to use a field for grouping, sorting, or setting criteria, but to exclude the field from the recordset, click the arrow in that field's Crosstab cell, and select "(not shown)" from the list, as shown above.

Creating Queries for Updating Records

When a query is based on either a single table or on two tables with a one-to-one relationship, all the fields in the query are updatable.

Queries which include more than one table, when some of the tables have a one-to-many relationship, are more difficult to design so that they are updatable. Usually, such a query could be designed to be updatable. This is also true of a query that includes an attached table, unless the attached table is a SQL database table with no unique index.

The easiest way of finding out whether you can update records, is to design the query, run it and try to change values in its various fields and also add data. If you can not change values in a field or add data, then you will be warned with an appropriate message on the Status bar.

All other types of queries, such as a Crosstab query, a query with totals, a query with Unique Values property set to Yes, a Union Query, a Pass-through query, a calculated or read-only field, can not be used to update data.

For example, if you try to change the first name under Employee ID from Smith to Smyth, you get the message "This Recordset is not updatable" on the Status bar at the bottom of the screen, as shown below.

Crosstab Query: Orders_Crosstab1																	
Order ID	Customer ID	Employee ID	Row Summary	Jan	Feb	Mar	Apr	May	Jun	Jul	Aug	Sep	Oct	Nov	Dec
94085VOR	VORT	A.D. Smith	1			1									
94097AVO	AVON	W.A. Brown	1		1										
94099BAR	BARR	S.F. Adams	1				1								
95002STO	STON	C.H. Wills	1				1								
95006PAR	PARK	A.D. Smith	1						1						
95010WES	WEST	W.A. Brown	1						1						
95018GLO	GLOW	L.S. Stevens	1							1					
95025SIL	SILV	S.F. Adams	1							1					
95029WOR	WORM	C.H. Wills	1								1				
95039EAL	EALI	A.D. Smith	1							1					
95045HIR	HIRE	W.A. Brown	1									1			
95051EUR	EURO	L.S. Stevens	1								1				
95064AVO	AVON	S.F. Adams	1										1		

Record: 1 of 13

This Recordset is not updatable.

Creating Action Queries

You can create *Action Queries* in the same way as Select Queries. Action Queries are used to make bulk changes to data rather than simply displaying data. For this reason, Action Queries can be dangerous for the novice, simply because they change your database.

There are four different types of Action Queries, with the following functions:

Type of Query	Function
Append query	Adds records from one or more tables to another table or tables.
Delete query	Deletes records from a table or tables.
Make-table query	Creates a new table from all or part of another table or tables.
Update query	Changes the data in a group of records

To quickly create an Action query which moves old orders to an Old Orders Archive table, click first the Queries button, then the **New** button on the Database window. Next, click the **Query Wizards** button on the New Query dialogue box and choose **Archive Query** from the list of Wizards in the Query Wizards dialogue box, as shown on the composite screen dump below.

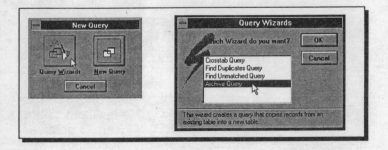

On pressing the **OK** button, the following dialogue box appears on the screen:

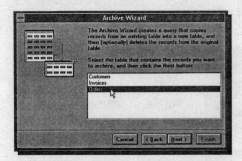

To create a new table from data held in the Orders table that will contain all the fields in that table, select from the displayed list the Orders table and click the **Next** button.

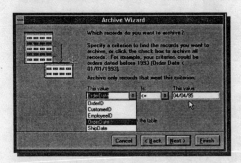

In the dialogue box displayed next, select the OrderDate field from the list in the first box, then type the date 04/04/95 in the third box. Clicking the **Next** button displays the next dialogue box, shown below, with all the records that will be archived.

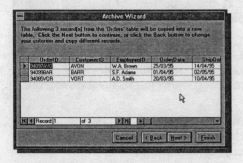

When you click **Next** again, Access asks you whether these records should be deleted from the original table after they have been archived (or copied).

Obviously the answer to this is **Yes** since we would like to form a new table into which all the old orders, placed during the previous financial year, are to be transferred.

You are then asked to name your new table; we chose to call it 'Old Orders Archive'. Finally, clicking the **Finish** button causes Access to carry out your wishes, but giving you ample warning before changing your data. If you choose to go ahead, Access places two new queries in the Query list, as shown here. These have an exclamation point attached to their icon so that you don't run them inadvertently.

In all, there are four Action queries available in Access. Below we list these, together with their corresponding buttons on the Tool bar.

  The Append query, used to append (add) records from one table to another existing table.

  The Delete query, used to delete (remove) records that meet certain predefined criteria from a table.

  The Make-Table query, used to create a table by retrieving the records that meet certain criteria and using them to create a new table.

  The Update query, used to change data in existing tables, such as the cost per hour charged to your customers.

8. USING FORMS & REPORTS

We saw at the end of Chapter 4 how easy it was to create a single column form to view our Customers table. To see this again, open Adept1 and in the Database window click the Form button, then double-click on Form1, which should display the following:

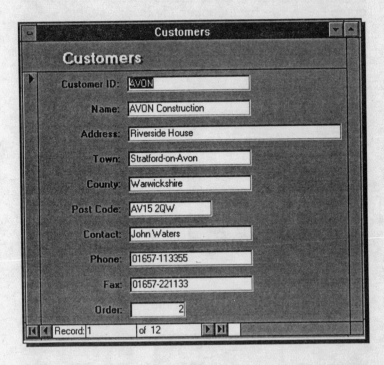

You can use forms to find, edit, and add data in a convenient manner. Access provides you with an easy way of designing various types of forms, some of which are discussed here. Forms look good on screen, but do not produce very good output on paper, whereas reports are designed to look good on paper, but do not necessarily look good on screen.

Using the Form Wizards

Using the Form Wizards, you can easily display data from either a table or a query in form view.

In the Database window, first click on the Form button, then click the **New** button which opens the New Form dialogue box in which you must choose either a table or a query on which to base the new form. In the screen dump below, we have chosen the Invoices table.

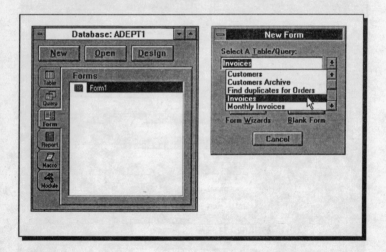

Next, click the **Form Wizards** button which displays the

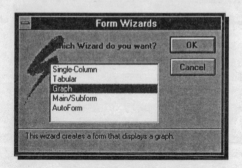

Form Wizards dialogue box, shown here. As you can see, there are 5 different types of forms available for you to choose from. Their function will be discussed shortly.

70

To continue with our exercise, we select Graph and click the **OK** button.

The next dialogue box, asks you for the fields that contain the data you want to graph. We chose InvoiceID and Amount, then clicked the **Next** button.

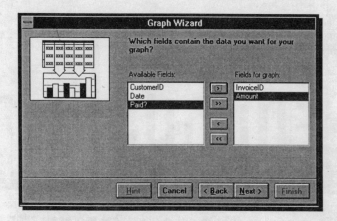

This opens another dialogue box in which you are asked to specify the way you want to calculate the totals for each category on your graph. Accept the default selection and click the **Next** button. You are now asked to select the type of graph, as shown below.

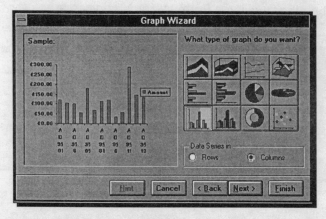

Again, accepting the default choice and clicking the **Finish** button, displays the following screen:

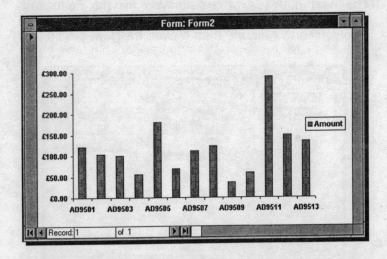

It is as easy as that to get a graphical representation of the amounts involved in each of your invoices. When you try to close this application, you will be asked whether you would like to save the changes to that form. Answering **Yes**, displays a dialogue box for you to type the name of the form. We have called this form 'Invoice amounts'.

The other available Form Wizards choices are:

Type of Form	Function
Single-Column	Displays fields in a single column.
Tabular	Displays each record as a row of fields.
Graph	Displays data graphically.
Main/Subform	Displays a form that contains another form. This form allows data from related tables to be viewed at the same time.
AutoForm	Displays a simple form automatically.

Customising a Form:

You can customise a form by changing the appearance of text, data, and any other attributes. To have a look at some of these options, double click on Form1 to display the Customers form, then click the Design View button on the Tool bar.

What appears on your screen is shown below:

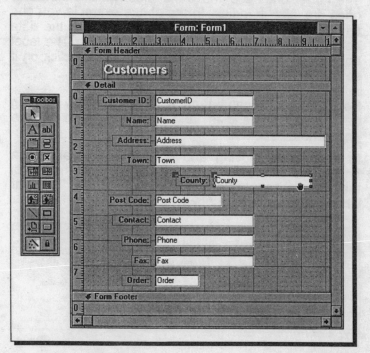

As you can see, a form in Design View is made up of boxes attached to a grid. Clicking at the County box, for example, causes markers to appear around it as shown above. When the mouse pointer is then placed within either the label box or data box, it changes to a hand which indicates that you can drag the box to a new position, as we have done above. This method moves both label and data boxes together.

If you look more closely at the markers around the label and data boxes, you will see that they are of different size, as shown below.

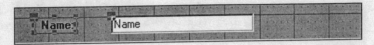

The larger ones are 'move' handles, while the smaller ones are 'size' handles. In the above example you can use the 'move' handles of either the label or the data box to move one independently of the other. The label box can also be sized. To size the data box, click on it so that the markers appear around it.

Boxes on a form can be made larger by simply pointing to the sizing handles and dragging them in the appropriate direction.

In addition to moving and enlarging label and data boxes, you can further customise a form with the use of the various new buttons that appear on the Tool bar when in Design View, shown below.

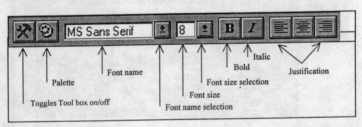

Do try and experiment with moving and sizing label and data boxes and also increasing their font size. If you don't like the result, simply don't save it. Skills gained here will be used in Report design.

The Toolbox can be used to either design a form from scratch (a task beyond the scope of this book), or add to it, such as a Combo (drop-down) box. The function of each tool on the Toolbox is listed on the next page.

The Toolbox

The Toolbox can be used to add items to a Form or Report. The function of each tool is listed below.

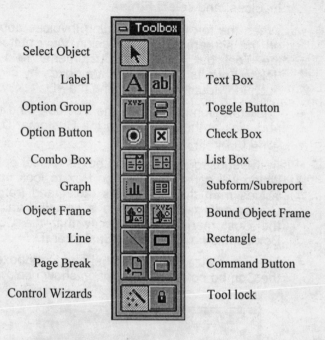

Select Object		
Label		Text Box
Option Group		Toggle Button
Option Button		Check Box
Combo Box		List Box
Graph		Subform/Subreport
Object Frame		Bound Object Frame
Line		Rectangle
Page Break		Command Button
Control Wizards		Tool lock

As an example of using the Toolbox, let us assume that we would like to use Form1 to enter new data into our Invoices table, but with the ability of selecting the CustomerID field from a drop-down menu - a Combo box.

To achieve the above, execute the following steps:

- On the Database window first click the Form button followed by the **New** button.

- In the New Form dialogue box select Invoices as the table on which to base the new Form, and click the **Form Wizards** button.

- In the following displayed dialogue boxes, select Single-Column, then choose all the fields from the Invoices table accept the Embossed style, and click the **Next** button.

- Give as the title of your form the name Adding Invoices, and select **Finish**.

- When the form entitled Adding Invoices appears on the screen, click the Design View button on the Tool bar, click the CustomerID field and delete both its Label and Data boxes by clicking each individually and pressing the <Del> key.

- Click the Combo Box on the Toolbox, and point and click at the area where the CustomerID field used to be on the form.

- In the subsequent dialogue boxes, select options which will cause the Combo Box to look up the values from the Customers table, and from the CustomerID field and store a selected value in the CustomerID field. Specify that the Combo Box should have the label Customer ID:.

- Move and size both the Label and Data boxes of the Combo box into the position shown below.

- Click the Form View button on the Toolbar, followed by the New button, both of which are shown below. The entry form should now look as follows:

- Use the **File, Save Form As** command to name this form Add Invoice.

From now on, whenever you want to add a new invoice to the Invoices table, use the Add Invoice form from the Database window, then click the New Form button on the Tool bar to display an empty form. Next, type in the relevant information in the appropriate data boxes on the form, but when you come to fill in the Customer ID field, click instead the down arrow against its data box to display the drop-down menu. Select one of the existing customers on the list, and click the Next Form button on the Tool bar.

Try the above procedure with the following details:

```
AD9514    WEST      28/10/95      £140
```

then verify that indeed the information has been recorded by double-clicking the Invoices table on the Database window.

Using the Report Wizards

We will use the skills gained in manipulating Forms in Design View to produce an acceptable report created by the Report Wizards.

To produce a report of the Unpaid Invoices query, click the Report button on the Database window and select the Unpaid Invoices query in the New Report dialogue box. The steps for this procedure are identical to those used to produce a new form.

Next, click the **Report Wizards** button and select the Tabular report from the displayed 7 types of reports (the last one of these is the MS Word Mail Merge report, but to see it you must scroll down the list).

Now, select all the fields (except for the Paid? field) which are to appear on your report and click the **Next** button, then select the InvoiceID field as the sort field, and accept all subsequent default settings. The report is created for you as follows:

Unpaid Invoices

19-Jun-95

Order ID	Amount	Invoice No	Name
		£120.84 AD9501	VORTEX Co. Ltd
		£99.32 AD9503	BARROWS Associates
95002STO		£55.98 AD9504	STONEAGE Ltd
95006PAR		£180.22 AD9505	PARKWAY Gravel
95010WES		£68.52 AD9506	WESTWOOD Ltd
95018GLO		£111.56 AD9507	GLOWORM Ltd
95029WOR		£35.87 AD9509	WORMGLAZE Ltd
95039EAL		£58.95 AD9510	EALING Engines Design
95045HIR		£290.00 AD9511	HIRE Service Equipment
95051EUR		£150.00 AD9512	EUROBASE Co. Ltd
95064AVO		£135.00 AD9513	AVON Construction

£1,306.26

78

Obviously this report is not quite acceptable. The problem is mainly the fact that all text fields are left justified within their columns, while numerical fields are right justified. Don't worry that the first two invoices don't appear to have an order associated with them; the orders for these were removed from the query when we formed the Old Orders Archive.

Returning to the report itself, what we would like to do is display it in Design View so that we can change the position of the numeric fields. To do this, use the **View, Toolbars** command, highlight the Report Design item in the **Toolbars** list of the displayed dialogue box and press the **Show** button, followed by the **Close** button. This displays an additional Tool bar which allows you access to the Design View button. Clicking this button displays the Report as follows:

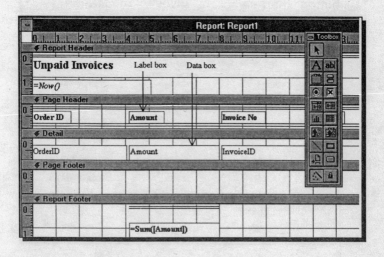

Use the mouse to move the Amount data box, the =Sum([Amount]) data box and the double lines above it to the left, and then right justify the text in the Amount label and data boxes and the formula at the bottom of the screen, as shown on the next page.

The corresponding report is now as follows:

Unpaid Invoices

19-Jun-95

Order ID	Amount	Invoice No	Name
95002STO	£120.84	AD9501	VORTEX Co. Ltd
95006PAR	£103.52	AD9502	AVON Construction
95010WES	£99.32	AD9503	BARROWS Associates
95018GLO	£55.98	AD9504	STONEAGE Ltd
95025SIL	£180.22	AD9505	PARKWAY Gravel
95029WOI	£68.52	AD9506	WESTWOOD Ltd
95039EAL	£111.56	AD9507	GLOWORM Ltd
95045HIR	£123.45	AD9508	SILVERSMITH Co
95051EUR	£35.87	AD9509	WORMGLAZE Ltd
95064AVC	£58.95	AD9510	EALING Engines Design

£958.23

This layout is obviously far more acceptable than that of the original report created by the Report Wizards.

We hope we have covered enough features of the program in this book and given you the foundations needed to make you want to explore Access more fully.

INDEX

NOTES

COMPANION DISC OFFER

COMPANION DISCS for all books (other than this book and the UNIX book), written by the same author(s) and published by BERNARD BABANI (publishing) LTD, are available and are listed at the front of this book. Such books contain many pages of file/program listings and there is no reason why you should spend hours typing such information into your computer, unless you wish to do so, or need the practice. COMPANION DISCS are available in both 3.5-inch and 5.25-inch formats and come with all the example listings.

ORDERING INSTRUCTIONS

To obtain your copy of the companion disc, fill in the order form below, enclose a cheque (payable to **P.R.M. Oliver**) or a postal order, and send it to the address given below. Make sure you fill in your name and address and specify the book number, title and the disc size in your order.

Book No.	Book Name	Unit Price	Total Price
BP		£3.50	
BP		£3.50	
BP		£3.50	
Name .... Address		Sub-total	£.............
		P & P (@ 45p/disc)	£.............
Disc Format 3.5-inch....... 5.25-inch......		Total Due	£.............
Send to: P.R.M. Oliver, CSM, Pool, Redruth, Cornwall, TR15 3SE			